Read, Recite, and Write

LIMERICKS

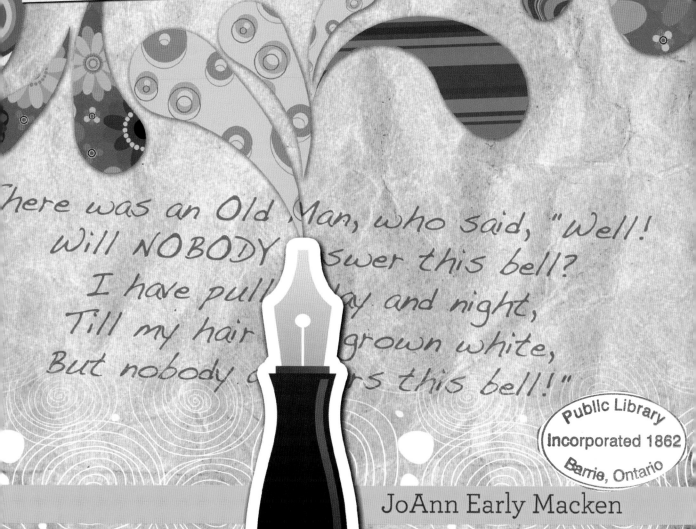

There was an Old Man, who said, "Well!
Will NOBODY answer this bell?
    I have pulled day and night,
    Till my hair has grown white,
But nobody answers this bell!!"

JoAnn Early Macken

Author
JoAnn Early Macken

Publishing plan research and development
Reagan Miller

Project coordinator
Kelly Spence

Editor
Anastasia Suen

Proofreader and indexer
Wendy Scavuzzo

Design
Margaret Amy Salter

Photo research
Margaret Amy Salter

Prepress technician
Margaret Amy Salter

Print and production coordinator
Margaret Amy Salter

Photographs and illustrations
Shutterstock: serjio74: page 10
Wikimedia Commons: Edward Lear: pages 4 (bottom left),
    6 (middle left), and 12 (middle); Wilhelm Marstrand: page
    6 (middle right)
Other images by Shutterstock

JoAnn Early Macken is the author of *Write a Poem Step by Step*
(Earlybird Press), five picture books, and 125 nonfiction books for
young readers. Her poems appear in several children's magazines
and anthologies. JoAnn has taught writing at four Wisconsin
colleges. She speaks about poetry and writing to students,
teachers, and adult writers at schools, libraries, and conferences.
You can visit her web site at www.joannmacken.com.

Library and Archives Canada Cataloguing in Publication

CIP available at Library and Archives Canada

Library of Congress Cataloging-in-Publication Data

CIP available at Library of Congress

Crabtree Publishing Company

Printed in Canada/032014/BF20140212

www.crabtreebooks.com 1-800-387-7650

Published in Canada
Crabtree Publishing
616 Welland Ave.
St. Catharines, Ontario
L2M 5V6

Published in the United States
Crabtree Publishing
PMB 59051
350 Fifth Avenue, 59th Floor
New York, New York 10118

Published in the United Kingdom
Crabtree Publishing
Maritime House
Basin Road North, Hove
BN41 1WR

Published in Australia
Crabtree Publishing
3 Charles Street
Coburg North
VIC 3058

Contents

Chapter 1: What Is a Limerick?

A limerick is a silly poem with five lines. In this book, you will learn how to write these fun poems. The lines in a limerick follow a special pattern:

-Lines 1, 2, and 5 **rhyme**
-Lines 3 and 4 rhyme

Reading other poems is a good way to learn how to write one. Reciting a silly poem aloud can help you, too. In this book, you will read and recite some very silly poems!

Limerick History

No one knows when the first limerick was written. These poems have the same name as a city in Ireland. But did the poems begin there? Why were they named after it? No one knows.

What we do know is when the first limerick was printed on paper. It was in 1820 in England. After that, Edward Lear wrote a book of limericks. He called it, *A Book of Nonsense*. It came out in 1846.

Lear's book was a huge success. People have been writing their own limericks ever since. Now it's your turn!

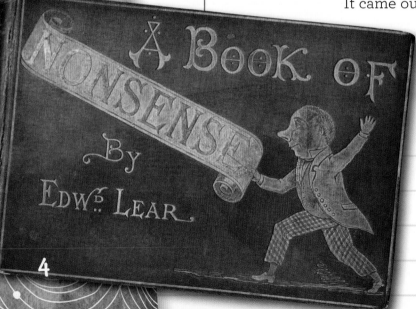

Prose vs. Drama vs. Poetry

In literature, we use different names to talk about the way words are used. As you can see in the examples below, the same story can be told in many different ways.

Drama

TIME: a long time ago.
PLACE: on the island of Crete.
[The YOUNG LADY is in bed. She opens her eyes.]
YOUNG LADY: It's morning.
[The YOUNG LADY leans over the edge of the bed.]
YOUNG LADY: Time to get up!
[The YOUNG LADY stands on her head next to the bed.]
YOUNG LADY: I have to keep my feet clean!

Prose

Once upon a time in the country of Crete, there lived a young lady who was exceedingly neat. She was so very neat that when she got out of bed she did something quite strange. She stood on her head to keep her feet clean.

Poetry

There was a young lady of Crete
Who was so exceedingly neat,
When she got out of bed,
She stood on her head
To make sure of not soiling her feet.
—Author Unknown

We use sentences to tell a story in **prose**. When a story is performed as a play, it is called a **drama**. Can you see the stage directions? They let the actors know when and where things happen.

The third example is a **poem**. A poem uses short **phrases**, or groups of words, to tell a story or share a feeling.

Writing Your Own Limerick

Limericks are silly and fun. The characters in these silly poems try to do impossible things.

A limerick is short. You won't have room to tell the whole story. You only have five lines. Not five sentences, but five lines. Most limericks are written as sentences broken into lines.

How much can you say in a sentence or two? You can share a short look at a zany situation. You can show us a ridiculous character. You can use silly words and make us laugh.

Edward Lear

Edward Lear wrote many limericks for his friends and their children. He was born in England in 1812. Lear was the second youngest of 21 children!

As a child, Edward was often sick. At 16, he earned money by drawing birds and animals. He wrote limericks and drew sketches for them when he was 20. Later, he traveled around the world. He wrote, drew, and sold artwork to earn a living.

Five Steps to Writing

1. Pre-writing: Brainstorm new ideas. Write every one down, even if it seems as though it might not work.

2. Drafting: Your first copy can be sloppy. You can always fix it later.

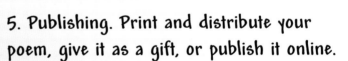

3. Revising: Use input from other writers to make your poem better.

4. Editing: Check for spelling, grammar, and punctuation.

5. Publishing. Print and distribute your poem, give it as a gift, or publish it online.

About This Book

In this book, you'll learn about one type of poem: the limerick.

Literature Links explore the tools that all types of literature use.

Poetry Pointers explain the parts that are special to poetry.

Thinking Aloud sections include discussion questions, brainstorming tips, graphic organizers, and examples of students' writing.

Now It's Your Turn! gives you tips on how to write your very own limerick.

Chapter 2: Writing a Place Name Limerick

Are you ready to write a limerick? In this chapter, you will read, write, and recite limericks that name a place. Many limericks begin with "a person from a place." Some place names are regular names. Others are funny. They might even be made up!

There was an old man from Peru
Who dreamt he was eating his shoe.
He awoke in the night
In a terrible fright
And found it was perfectly true!
—Author Unknown

There was an old man of the North
Who fell into a basin of broth,
But a laudable cook
Fished him out with a hook,
Which saved that old man of the North.
—Edward Lear

Poetry Pointer: Rhyme

Listen for rhyme. You can hear it. Rhyming words sound different at the beginning, but alike at the end. What matters is the way the words are pronounced, not the way they are spelled. In the first poem, *Peru*, *shoe*, and *true* rhyme, and *night* rhymes with *fright*. In the second poem, *cook* rhymes with *hook*. In some limericks, especially those of Edward Lear, the last word in line 5 is the same as the last word in line 1.

Slant Rhyme

The right word is the word that says exactly what you mean. Sometimes, the right word does not quite rhyme. In the second poem, *North* does not quite rhyme with *broth*. That almost-rhyme is called **slant rhyme** or near rhyme.

When you write, try to balance the need for logic with the need to use the words that sound best. A better solution might be available if you keep looking. For example, Lear could have rhymed *North* with *forth* or *fourth*. He could have rhymed *broth* with *cloth* or *moth* or *sloth*. He could even have changed *broth* to *soup* or *stew*. He could have made up a place name and found a third rhyme for one of those words.

A five-line limerick uses the rhyme scheme: **aabba.**

Rhyme Schemes

A **rhyme scheme** is a way to describe a rhyming pattern. Each line is assigned a letter based on the last word in the line. All the lines that rhyme are given the same letter. When you hear a new rhyme, you use the next letter in the alphabet.

There was an old man of the North **a**
Who fell into a basin of broth, **a**
But a laudable cook **b**
Fished him out with a hook, **b**
Which saved that old man of the North. **a**
—Edward Lear

Literature Link: Setting

Setting is the place where a story happens. It also includes the time. Many limericks name the place that the character comes from. Can you spot the setting of the two limericks in this chapter?

Can you tell when the poem happened? Was it in the past, the present, or the future? The **tense** of the verbs is a good clue.

Thinking Aloud

To write about a place in a limerick, first you need to select a place. Then you need to find two words that rhyme with that place.

Trevor and his group made a list of places with two syllables. Then they brainstormed some rhyming words to use in lines 2 and 5.

Madrid	hid, skid, did, slid, forbid, squid, kid
Brazil	hill, chill, thrill, pill, wind mill, until, spill, still
Japan	man, fan, plan, tan, can, began, caravan
Des Plaines	brains, chains, explains, remains, trains, airplanes
St. Cloud	aloud, loud, crowd, proud, allowed, wowed
De Pere	hear, clear, cheer, tear, ear, fear, year, root beer, sincer

Write Your Own Place Name Limerick

Now It's Your Turn! First, you need to think of a place. Make a list of places you have visited or read about. You can also check an atlas, a globe, or a map. Think about making up a place name.

After you decide on a place name, you need to find two words that rhyme with it. *Fish Creek* rhymes with *speak*, *hide and seek*, and *unique*. *Mobile* rhymes with *kneel*, *oatmeal*, and *squeal*. Names such as Egypt or Mount Horeb might not have any usable rhymes.

The next step is to make your character move. Who is your character anyway?

What does he or she do?

Now you're ready to write your limerick.

Make a list of silly actions.

Trevor chose Des Plaines from the students' brainstorming list. He wrote this poem:

There once was a man from Des Plaines
who cared for a pack of Great Danes.
He walked them outdoors
in twos, threes, and fours
and said "I only mind when it rains."

Chapter 3: Writing an Animal Antics Limerick

In this chapter, you will read, write, and recite limericks about animal antics. Yes, you will write a poem about silly animals. Will the main character in the poem talk to silly animals? Or will the main character in the poem be a silly animal? Read on and find out!

There was an Old Man with a beard,
Who said, "It is just as I feared!
Two Owls and a Hen,
four Larks and a Wren
Have all built their nests in my beard!"
—Edward Lear

There was an old man of Dumbree
Who taught little owls to drink tea.
For he said, "To eat mice
Is not proper or nice,"
That amiable man of Dumbree.
—Edward Lear

Poetry Pointer: Rhythm and Meter

To **meter** means to measure. Poems with regular beats or **stressed** syllables—that is, a regular **rhythm**—are called metered or metric.

To find the beat, or stressed syllables, tap or clap along as you read. You should feel the emphasis, or stress, on the syllables written in CAPITAL letters.

This is what it looks like in a poem.

there WAS an old MAN with a BEARD,

who SAID, "it is JUST as i FEARED!

two OWLS and a HEN,

four LARKS and a WREN

have ALL built their NESTS in my BEARD!"

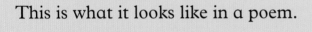

Listen for the repeating three-syllable rhythm pattern. You'll hear it in "an old MAN with a BEARD," "it is JUST as i FEARED," "and a HEN," and so on. That da da DUM pattern is common in limericks.

Notice the number of stressed syllables in each line. Lines 1, 2, and 5 each have three. Lines 3 and 4 each have two. Can you see the pattern in the second poem?

Literature Link: Description

Limericks are very short. There is not a lot of room for description. In the first poem in this chapter, Edward Lear names four specific types of birds: *Two Owls and a Hen, four Larks and a Wren.* These specific names give you a clear picture of the birds.

To make your poem clear, use words that are specific. Instead of *dog*, use *beagle*, *bulldog*, or *poodle.* Choose a specific *flower*, like a *daffodil*, a *rose*, or a *tulip.*

> Specific words help readers see what you mean.

Thinking Aloud

You don't have to start every poem with the words, "There was…" You can be more specific than that.

Kayla and her group brainstormed a list of first lines. For some, they used descriptions. For others, they used job titles.

A long-legged lion who paced

A veterinarian from France

A grumpy reporter from Maine

A hungry mosquito at sea

A brave kangaroo in a cave

A farmer from Saskatchewan

A black-and-white polka-dot cow

A second-grade teacher from Spain

A quiet fourth grader from Hobbs

A sleepy Canadian bear

What other first lines can you imagine?

Write Your Own Animal Antics Limerick

Now It's Your Turn! Are you ready to write a silly animal poem? You can use one of the first lines from Kayla's list or make a new list of your own. Invent your own characters and actions.

Kayla wrote this limerick. She included one of her favorite words.

A zookeeper, fond of a gnu,
let him wander around in a zoo
till he took a big munch
from a visitor's lunch
and started a hullabaloo.

15

Chapter 4: Writing a Foolish Character Limerick

Here come the fools! In this chapter, you will read, write, and recite limericks about a foolish character. These characters make us laugh when they do silly things.

There was a young lady of Ealing
Who had a peculiar feeling
That she was a fly
And wanted to try
To walk upside down on the ceiling.
—Author Unknown

There was an old person of Wilts
Who constantly walked upon stilts.
He wreathed them in lilies
And daffy-down-dillies,
That elegant person of Wilts.
—Edward Lear

Poetry Pointer: Alliteration

Are you ready to play with words? Can you write a line with words that all begin with the same sound? You can see *daffy-down-dillies* in the poem. This sound pattern is called **alliteration**.

There are some other sound patterns you can try. You may want to repeat the same consonant in another place. Have some of the words in a line end with the same consonant sound. You can also try putting it in the middle of several words in a line. Can you hear the *d* sound in *muddy bird feeder*? When consonants repeat in the middle or the end of several words in a line, it is called **consonance**.

If you try this with vowels, it is called **assonance**. You can see it in this line: "high-flying skydivers."

Literature Link: Characters

Many limericks begin with a simple character description: "There was an old man from _____," or "There once was a girl from _____." They might be referred to by their job. Often, they are just described as young or old. They are rarely given a name.

Actions tell us more than the descriptions. They show who the characters really are. What silly actions did you see in these two limericks? How did those actions tell you more about the characters?

17

Thinking Aloud

Devon's group brainstormed as they started to write. They wanted to show that their characters were silly. First, they made a list of silly actions they could write about.

goals or dreams

ridiculous jobs

impossible tasks

funny habits

Then they made a **cluster**.

To make a cluster, write the subject you want to explore in the center of the page and circle it. Then write a new word about that idea. Circle it and draw a line to connect it. As you think of more ideas, make the cluster bigger by adding new links.

The more specific you can be the better!

swim across an ocean

climb a mountain

dune sweeper

worm trainer

fly

sleep all day

goals or dreams

ridiculous jobs

impossible feats

wear a cloud

bird choir director

Silly Actions

eat a rainbow

ants

funny habits

always singing

collecting things

tap dancing around

pickle jars

freckles

Write Your Own Foolish Character Limerick

Now It's Your Turn! It's time to write about your fool! Just one reminder. The famous poet Edward Lear never made fun of specific people. When you write about a foolish character, try to be silly without being mean.

You could begin in one of these ways:

Think of a person you know. Exaggerate one feature or habit.

Use clustering to help you think up a new idea.

Use an idea from the students' cluster.

Devon wrote this limerick:

A brilliant boy from Beijing
collected small pieces of string,
rolled them up in a ball
in the summer and fall,
and unrolled it all in the spring.

Devon used alliteration in line 1. Could you do the same in your poem?

Chapter 5: Writing a Punch Line Limerick

Can you exaggerate? Can you play with words? Can you write silly nonsense? In this chapter, you can do all three! You will read, write, and recite limericks that tell a joke. The last line will be the **punch line**. That's because a punch line is the end of a joke.

A cheerful old bear at the zoo
Could always find something to do.
When it bored him to go
On a walk to and fro,
He reversed it and walked fro and to.
—Author Unknown

An oyster from Kalamazoo
Confessed he was feeling quite blue.
"For," says he, "as a rule,
When the weather turns cool,
I invariably get in a stew."
—Author Unknown

Poetry Pointer: Wordplay

Wordplay is just what it sounds like: fun with words. It might include **puns**, tongue twisters, or other clever phrases.

A pun is a joke in which words that sound alike are used in a new way. For example: "The baker really kneads [needs] the dough."

20

Tongue twisters have words with many sounds that are alike. "She sells seashells by the seashore." Tongue twisters can be very hard to say!

You can use a common saying for wordplay. In the first limerick example, the phrase "to and fro" is reversed to "fro and to."

In the second example, "in a stew" means in trouble. So does "in a pickle." Watch for other examples of wordplay as you read.

Literature Link: Word Choice
A limerick contains so few words that each one should be the best possible choice. How do you decide which words to use?

A word's meaning is the most important factor. Be sure that the words you choose mean what you intend to say.

Rhyme is also important. But be careful not to choose a rhyming word just because it rhymes. It has to make sense, too.

Rhythm also matters, but it does not have to be perfect. Changing the rhythm just a bit can make a poem more interesting.

Only use the words you need. (If the poem still makes sense without a word, then you don't really need it.)

Thinking Aloud

Nikki and her group brainstormed some common sayings. They wanted to play with them to see what they could come up with. They made a list of examples that might fit in a limerick:

saved by the bell

out of the blue

at the drop of a hat

under the weather

actions speak louder than words

hit the hay

pulling my leg

?

How can you play with one of these phrases? Can you add any others?

let sleeping dogs lie

Write Your Own Punch Line Limerick
Now It's Your Turn!

Are you ready to write a limerick that ends with a punch line? Here are some ways to begin:

Think of a pun or joke. See if you can fit it into the limerick form.

Make a list of words that include the same sound. Turn them into a tongue twister.

Start with one of the phrases from the students' brainstorming list. Choose rhymes for the words in the sayings.

? Look at each word carefully. Can you play with the sound or meaning?

Nikki wrote this limerick, which plays with the phrase *turned in*, or went to sleep.

You can use a word that not everyone knows. To be sure it has the meaning you want, look it up in a dictionary. To find another word that means almost the same thing, check a **thesaurus**. A thesaurus is a book with lists of words that are close in meaning.

A tumbler who lived in Green Bay
somersaulted around every day.
She stood on her head
when she turned in to bed.
In the morning, she turned out okay.

You could play with the same phrase. Write about someone who turns into, or becomes, something else.

23

Chapter 6: Writing a Silly Spelling Limerick

Are you ready to bend the rules? In this chapter, you will read, write, and recite limericks with silly spellings. The words you use will sound right. But the way you spell some of them won't be in any dictionary!

As you read the poems in this chapter, remember how a limerick uses rhyme. The words at the end of lines 1, 2, and 5 always rhyme with each other.

In these poems, the words at the end of lines 2 and 5 have silly spellings. So how will you say them? Make those words rhyme with the correctly spelled word at the end of line 1.

Making Up Silly Spellings

How can you make up silly spellings? In these poems, the author used the end of the place name for the rhyme.

A painter who came from Great Britain
Hailed a lady who sat with her knitain.
He remarked with a sigh,
"That park bench—well, I
Just painted it, right where you're sitain."
—Author Unknown

A trumpeter from Illinois
lent his trumpet one day to a bois
who tooted around
till he made a rude sound.
Said the trumpeter, "That's not a tois!"
—JoAnn Early Macken

In this poem, the word *Britain* rhymes with *knittin'* and *sittin'*. In both words, the final *g* was dropped to make the word rhyme. The next step was to make the spellings silly. The nonsense words *knitain* and *sitain* are spelled to end the same as *Britain*.

In this poem, the silent *s* at the end of Illinois is used for the silly spelling. (You say it like this: il-uh-NOY.) It rhymes with the words *boy* and *toy*. Change the spelling and a *boy* becomes a *bois* and a *toy* becomes a *tois*.

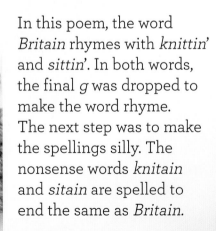

Poetry Pointer: Rhyming Dictionaries

A limerick needs two sets of rhyming words. One set (for lines 1, 2, and 5) needs three words. One set (for lines 3 and 4) needs two words.

That's a lot of rhyming words! You can use a **rhyming dictionary** to help you. A rhyming dictionary doesn't tell you what a word means. Look up a word and what will you see? It shows you a list of words that rhyme. The words in the list have the same sounds.

What Rhymes with *Blue?*

blew	crew	few	grew	moo	shoe
boo	cue	flew	hew	new	shoo
brew	dew	flu	hue	pew	shrew
chew	do	flue	Hugh	pooh	true
clue	drew	glue	Knew	queue	
coo	due	gnu	lieu	rue	
coup	ewe	goo	mew	screw	

A rhyming dictionary can help you, but it can also hurt you. Don't try to use every word you find. Not every word that rhymes will make sense. You have to figure out a way to connect the words you use. It works better when you know what you want to say first. Then you can find the right words to say it.

Literature Link: Conventions

Conventions are the rules. When you write, those rules tell you how to spell a word. They tell you when to add a period or a comma. They remind you to begin a sentence with a capital letter. They tell you which words to use.

In this chapter, you are going to break one of those rules. Silly spelling can make your poem silly, too. When you know the rules, you can break them on purpose for a laugh.

Thinking Aloud

Miguel and his group brainstormed a list of places with unusual spellings. Then they added rhyming words. They changed some of the spellings to match.

Place name	Rhyming words (correct spelling)
Arkansas	clas (claw), dras (draw), jas (jaw), gnas (gnaw), jigsas (jigsaw)
Timbuktu	zu (zoo), yu (you), gnu, flu, du (do), blu (blue), tru (true)
Seville	hille (hill), spille (spill), untille (until), windowsille (windowsill)
Belize	knize (knees), frize (freeze), squize (squeeze), chize (cheese)
Tangier	hier (hear or here), ier (ear), chier (cheer), clier (clear), pier
McLeod	creod (crowd), preod (proud), aleod (aloud), meeod (meowed)
Eau Claire	baire (bear or bare), whaire (where), waire (wear), chaire (chair)
Illinois	bois (boy), tois (toy), jois (joy), sois (soy), enjois (enjoy)
Pierre	hierre (here or hear), ierre (ear), chierre (cheer), clierre (clear)

Write Your Own Silly Spelling Limerick
Now It's Your Turn!

You have seen lots of silly spellings in this chapter. Now it's your turn to make some silly spellings of your own. First, you need a place to write about. You can use the name of a place you know. You could also start with one of the place names in Miguel's brainstorming list.

Miguel took a trip to Lake Superior. He learned that a Native American name for the lake is *Gitche Gumee*. He wrote this limerick using the spelling of the lake name. Then he changed the spelling of the words at the end of lines 2 and 5. He made those words match the place name.

A sailor who sailed Gitche Gumee
thought her sailboat was comfy and roomee.
But then one chilly day,
she sailed across a wide bay,
and she said, "This awful wind blows right throughmee."

In the next chapter, you can see how Miguel's classmates helped him revise his limerick.

Chapter 7: Revising Your Limerick

Congratulations! You have just completed the first two steps of writing. You brainstormed new ideas, then you used them to write your first draft. Now you are ready for the next two steps: revising and editing. Use this checklist as a guide.

Yes/No	Limerick Revision Checklist
	1. Do the rhyming words rhyme well?
	2. Does the rhythm match from line to line?
	3. Can something repeat for a greater effect?
	4. Did you play with words to make the poem funny or silly?
	5. Is the description specific?

Group Help

One good way to revise your poem is to share it with a group. Give each person a copy. Ask them to write their comments on it. Ask one person to read your poem aloud. Listen for any places where the reader stumbles with rhythm and rhyme. Give the others a chance to speak before you say anything about your work.

Then move to the next writing step. Did they see anything you need to edit? Are there any spelling, grammar, or punctuation errors? (Even silly spelling words need to be spelled so they match.)

Take time to think about every comment. Then use the ones that make the most sense to you.

Miguel gave his group a copy of his silly spelling poem. They thought that Miguel's silly spelling helped make his limerick funnier. They also commented on the spelling and word choice.

Trevor pointed out that Miguel could use the whole spelling of –*umee*, not just –*ee*, at the ends of lines 2 and 5. Kayla suggested changing *chilly* to *cold*. That would make the rhythm of line 3 better. Devon suggested something different for line 3. "If you take out the word *then*, it still says the same thing. We see what happened next."

Nikki found a way to shorten line 4. "You can say *crossed* instead of *sailed across*." Kayla said, "You could also cut *she* from the last line." Miguel decided to use a more specific word to describe the wind in line 5. This is how he revised his poem:

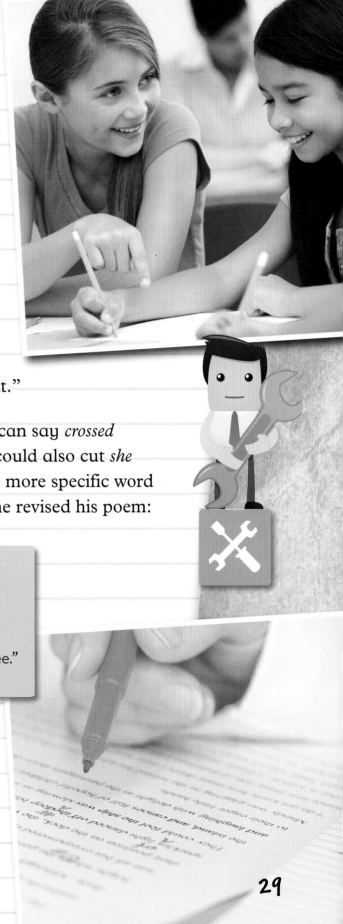

A sailor who sailed Gitche Gumee
thought her sailboat was comfy and rumee.
But one chilly day,
she crossed a wide bay
and said, "This bitter wind blows right thrumee."

Helping others revise and edit their poems can help you, too. When you read others' work, look for the positive. Point out what works well. Be supportive. Writing is not easy, and sharing can be even harder! If you don't understand something, ask a question.

Chapter 8: Performing a Poem

The final step of writing is publishing your work. After you finish the final copy of your poem, you can share it with others. You can read your limerick aloud to a group. You can perform your own poem!

Limericks are silly poems. That makes them fun to read aloud. Be sure to practice ahead of time. Actors do that and so do comedians. How you say the lines can make the poem even funnier.

If you can, make a recording. When you play it back, notice what worked well. Did you speak clearly? Did you emphasize the rhythm and the rhyme?

Limerick Day

Edward Lear was born on May 12. You can celebrate his birthday. Make a birthday cake and read some limericks aloud. Take turns and have fun!

Learning More

Books

A Book of Nonsense by Edward Lear. Wordsworth Editions Ltd. (1999)

Grimericks by Susan Pearson. Two Lions (2013)

Limericks by Valerie Bodden. Creative Education (2010)

Pocketful of Nonsense compiled by James Marshall. HMH Books for Young Readers (2003)

Write a Poem Step by Step by JoAnn Early Macken. Earlybird Press (2012)

Websites

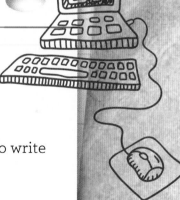

How to Write a Limerick by Kenn Nesbitt:
www.poetry4kids.com/blog/lessons/how-to-write-a-limerick/

This fun website provides a simple overview for young poets to write their own limericks.

Limericks from Scholastic:
www.scholastic.com/content/collateral_resources/pdf00premium/17/0439560217_e003.pdf

A helpful overview for working on limerick-writing in student groups.

How to Write a Limerick by Bruce Lansky:
www.gigglepoetry.com/poetryclass/limerickcontesthelp.html

Step-by-step instructions on writing limericks.

Glossary

Note: Some boldfaced words are defined where they appear in the book.

alliteration A series of words that begin with the same sound

assonance A series of words with the same vowel sound

cluster A brainstorming technique that links related words together

consonance A series of words which have the same consonant sound in the middle and/or at the end

drama A story meant to be performed as a play

prose The language we speak and write every day

rhyme Identical sounds at the ends of words

rhyme scheme A system of describing the rhyming pattern of a poem or stanza

rhythm A pattern of regular sounds in a series of words

setting Time and place

stressed Emphasized

tense The form of a verb that shows time as past, present, or future

Index